Penumbra

Kate Behrens was born in 1959 with her late twin Sophie. Two Rivers Press published *The Beholder* (2012) and *Man with Bombe Alaska* (2016). She lives in Oxfordshire and has one child.

Other books by the same author

The Beholder (Two Rivers Press, 2012)
Man with Bombe Alaska (Two Rivers Press, 2016)

Also by Two Rivers poets

David Attwooll, *The Sound Ladder* (2015)
Adrian Blamires, *The Pang Valley* (2010)
Adrian Blamires & Peter Robinson (eds.), *The Arts of Peace* (2014)
David Cooke, *A Murmuration* (2015)
Terry Cree, *Fruit* (2014)
Claire Dyer, *Eleven Rooms* (2013)
Claire Dyer, *Interference Effects* (2016)
John Froy, *Sandpaper & Seahorses* (2018)
A. F. Harrold, *The Point of Inconvenience* (2013)
Ian House, *Nothing's Lost* (2014)
Gill Learner, *The Agister's Experiment* (2011)
Gill Learner, *Chill Factor* (2016)
Sue Leigh, *Chosen Hill* (2018)
Becci Louise, *Octopus Medicine* (2017)
Mairi MacInnes, *Amazing Memories of Childhood, etc.* (2016)
Steven Matthews, *On Magnetism* (2017)
Henri Michaux, *Storms under the Skin* translated by Jane Draycott (2017)
Tom Phillips, *Recreation Ground* (2012)
John Pilling & Peter Robinson (eds.), *The Rilke of Ruth Speirs:
    New Poems, Duino Elegies, Sonnets to Orpheus & Others* (2015)
Peter Robinson, *English Nettles and Other Poems* (2010)
Peter Robinson (ed.), *Reading Poetry: An Anthology* (2011)
Peter Robinson (ed.), *A Mutual Friend: Poems for Charles Dickens* (2012)
Peter Robinson, *Foreigners, Drunks and Babies: Eleven Stories* (2013)
Lesley Saunders, *Cloud Camera* (2012)
Lesley Saunders, *Nominy-Dominy* (2018)
Robert Seatter, *The Book of Snow* (2016)
Jack Thacker, *Handling* (2018)
Susan Utting, *Fair's Fair* (2012)
Susan Utting, *Half the Human Race* (2017)
Jean Watkins, *Scrimshaw* (2013)
Jean Watkins, *Precarious Lives* (2018)

Penumbra

Kate Behrens

First published in the UK in 2019 by Two Rivers Press
7 Denmark Road, Reading RG1 5PA
www.tworiverspress.com

© Kate Behrens 2019

The right of the poet to be identified as the author of this work has been asserted by her in accordance with the Copyright, Designs and Patents Act of 1988.

All rights reserved. No part of this publication may be reproduced, stored in or introduced into a retrieval system, or transmitted, in any form, or by any means (electronic, mechanical, photocopying, recording or otherwise) without the prior written permission of the publisher.

ISBN 978-1-909747-46-3

1 2 3 4 5 6 7 8 9

Two Rivers Press is represented in the UK by Inpress Ltd and distributed by NBNi.

Cover illustration by Sally Castle
Text and cover design by Nadja Guggi and typeset in Janson and Parisine

Printed and bound in Great Britain by Imprint Digital, Exeter

Acknowledgements

Some of these poems, or their earlier versions, have appeared in *Poetry Salzburg Review* no. 32, *Stand* volume 15, *University of Reading Creative Arts Anthology* 2017, *Blackbox Manifold* issue 18 and *The High Window* autumn 2017. I am grateful to their editors. Many thanks to Peter Robinson for his patience as editor of this book, also to Jack Thacker, Dennis Nurkse, Ian House, Susan Utting, Antonia Monson, Steven Matthews, Jack Harber and Peter Foster for their variously invaluable contributions to its making.

*To Jack, with love
and to the memory of my father,
Tim Behrens 1937–2017*

Contents

I

Circolo Night | 3
Another Era | 4
Hotel Room at Night | 5
Inside the Lens | 6
Aeroplane Trails at Dusk | 7

II

The Hottest Night | 11
Robin | 12
I Sat in the Chair for Measuring Breaths | 13
Hidden Birds | 14
After Seeing my Father Dead | 15
Pigeons | 16
One Form of Freedom | 17
Fallow Deer at Stonor | 19
Two Stages | 20
Pigeon | 22
The Accomplice | 23
Thrush | 24
At Last | 25
On the Edge of the Field | 26
Tiny Thistles | 27

III

Tracks on the Skin | 31
Glimmer | 32
Beech Wood | 33
Mr Charles Brown and his Horse, Back from Market | 34

Apologia | 35
Delusions of Grandeur | 36
Dream Flight | 37
Good Dream | 38
Stamped on the Day | 39
Under the Supermoon | 40
From Surd to Love | 41
Before & Thirty Years On | 42
Falling Out of Love (Towards Love) | 43
Leo | 44

IV

True Story | 49
Stopped | 50
Girl on Motorway Bus | 51
The Festival Poet | 52
Guests at a Book Launch | 53
At the Plant Stall, February 2017 | 54
City Fragments, February 2018 | 55
Two Writers Walking | 55
Lights in the Departure Lounge | 56
After the Service | 57

V

Outside a Florist's, mid-December | 61
The Rabbit I Tamed Yawns | 62
From Watlington Hill | 63
Between the Lines (Traces from a Small Tractor) | 64
The Sponsored Ride | 65
Dead Tree Amongst Memorials | 66
After Restoring the Name on a Grave | 67
Notes from Aldeburgh Beach | 68
In Gratitude | 70

I

Circolo Night
i.m. L.

Multi-purpose, they'd string it with chains
of gritty paper, hurl us some phrases.
'*Siamo pazzi d'allegria*'...
Blue-gold under white neon strips,
Anselmo's sax riffed giant lilies
with dad, Enzo, light on the squeezebox.

The miniature grandparents trotted,
swept through confetti on field-stiffened arms.
Outside, bats nibbled at street light.

Cicadas under blued lime cliffs
incanted in balloons of heat
rising up through dried grasses

to tied-up dogs barking their hearts out
above our track,
where he would startle me –
startle me from childhood.

Circolo (It.); club
Siamo pazzi d'allegria (It.); we are crazy with joy

Another Era

Jellifying autostradas and, shirtless, Dad joined in
with Me and Bobby McGee, loading on bomblets of promise

that scattered from tips into ditches, once, into petrol pumps.
Ginger fingers kept time, slap-slapping the wheel as we screamed

'freedom's just another word for nothing left to lose',

till home, he skimmed records like frisbees, or hipslams on bar
    slot-machines
meant the mood flipped on one more grappa.

That pheromone cocktail, it stains us so like desire.

He stole us a tree for Christmas, passed the fags and fiasco,
boiled an egg when he had to, hummed 'You're a Big Girl Now'
and built us a wall of logs.
Because it calmed him, he built us a wall of logs –

followed the women out of the picture, returned to fall
in love with another girl. Or triangle. Always
unravelled

stories like wool with jokes woven in. Show me your art books
    (focusing),
Babbo of back then. Hum me 'Der Friede sei mit dir'.

You were in love with that leaver waving his fag-end or paintbrush,
everything he deemed cool, serious, or framed
with his body.

Hotel Room at Night
i.m. S.B.

'There' was Nicosia
but felt from isolation,
like Perseid's silvers tonight,
sensed behind a lagging of cloud.

We were eight-year-old twins,
the walls were white and growing
on absence.

I was trained on your flight,
already bereft, as we
listened to distances,

I, to you spinning through space
now that your mind was re-broken,
both, to glittering cars

that sighed and hushed like sea
your 'joy-ride' man had swum.

Unseen, those meteors
flash through *'a rareness forsaken'*
and in the silence of fallen light.

Inside the Lens

Tourists repeat, pixelating
where I drifted in,
their chopped-at-the-neck haircuts
a blue-black tilted backwards,
pyramidal rictuses
like families we lost.

Bell towers satirise
childhood's campaniles.
No echo chambers fling
bursts of wing beats here.
No purple-orange centres
pulse street shadows thrown
to slat, through blinded windows,
hotel counterpanes.

No loners, drifters, pray.
No slowness slows their pain
in the city. Or scintillates
riparian scribbles seen
from listing hairpin bends.

I'm mere approximations.
The sky: acraze with jets.

Aeroplane Trails at Dusk

Nobody stands under those three lines.
One's more a graze: static, orange, angled
strangely to the others. All enclose
us as we once were, and pared down
to fantastic optimism; the moon
we drew, slowly.

II

The Hottest Night

Inside has magnified
the louder quiet we create
to void.
Dark swells…
swells what can't be said.

Flowers thread breathed-on trees
with piquancy; syringa,
brighter than the moonlit field.
Blue cows yield to sleep, groan
like old men.

No scents reach your flightless lingering,
belligerent bird – our blood.
You suffer: I'm afraid.

What you were still stains this air,
like coloured glass.
But I digress.

Robin

Those wings are too personal.
Dreamy, he tucks his head into centimetres
of self. His signature is limited
to a frozen drift the wind has sculpted to peaks.
The enemy lands, fat and sleek as a drone,
to peck at him. Ours hesitates, hops twice.
Looks up at my face behind towering glass, sways,
turns his beak wingwards. He's walnut-sized, the world s
melodrama's fading. He slips under
a litter of leaves, one snowflake on his breast.

I Sat in the Chair for Measuring Breaths

high over the bay
of sparkling tomorrows,
scribbles in blue, primrose,

thinking *that* 'you' was extinct,
as you flickered through imagined
bars, or pissed
between my own shock-numbed fingers,
ripped the cannula out again,
shrieked at being turned.

You surface through the poisons
pleading for a drink.

Younger and younger, your face
purifies, comes true
for the woman seated there,
a stranger who appeared
looking like your daughter.

I see you scoop the air
with the side of your hand,
ask, *were you warm enough
in that chair?*

Hidden Birds

The sky's steel door slides open,
lawlessly dumbs down
their points of reference.
This glow is abnormal for night,
this quiet, an unwanted island
of closed, imperilled eyes.
Imagine their feathers' aeration,
how slowed-down heartbeats convey
the drama-less slopes of torpor,
the beaks' minute emanations,
unfeeling, from wood,
from burnt air.
Stifled from kisses of snow,
the earth has sucked out thought
to all but the thought-free
exactitudes in not dying.

After Seeing my Father Dead

Walking back, we follow the coastline's curves.
Roadside flowers have turned into mementos
positioned round the sealed and cleaned-up holes
he vanished through (his were not those angel-lips,
how dare they steal his complications, unholy pain!)
Now there's a line of aloe veras, frozen gesticulations
registering as other starving beings;
then, red and green identical twin blocks.
Still, his world is fast turning edgeless,
baffles without the government of
those sudden drops of his.
Baffles with this outliving love,
wiser than us.

Pigeons

Blue pavements
emptied of people
enthralled by each other.
Buildings are spectacular shields.
Birding, I note
their secret doings,
like heartbreak suddenly spilt,
banal, on glitter.
How sure they are
of what replaces myth.

One Form of Freedom

Lighting the wind with wisteria stems
flames up easy, spins from fine grain
to exhilarate a gaseous rage
grief's collected; burning statements
this early in mourning
are not about you, just symptoms.

*

As if one might halt
the unalterable drift
of the recently dead

so you'd stop spinning,
bubble-man,
as uncontainable
now as then…

*

No trace of angels in an unsigned sky
of slammed-into trails, several unlikely angles,
streaks, under cobalt, of phthalo turquoise
like you'd've painted, maybe with fantasy add-ons.

We sought out from life tricks that tranquilise
but from opposite ends of the spectrum; yours,
one form of freedom in wild flights from time,
mine, shackled to information…

*

Black. Wind. Stars.
Daphne Odorata.
Though the bonfire's out
I'm digging over it.
Even stone-cold ashes
can be blown alive
like a loved one's long
self-annihilation.
Daphne Odorata
(mother and father in the dark):
guide me to my bed.

Fallow Deer at Stonor

They might've been scissored out
from January clouds
or punched through the rhythms
of near-rhyming haunches, flanks,
chestnuts, mottled rust.

Lain up on a leaf-fall circle
these two are whiter than angels,
tamed by that artificial
frame. Their backdrop is gold
as the Wilton Dyptich.
Dama dama: the human drama.

Two Stages

Given reactant layers fused into your own
which is the dad I should mourn

...if you're listening out there...?

'*Joder!*' Your eyes are rolling.
Etiolated hands,
palms up in supplication, float
up and down.

The un-deadness (almost a smell)
is no pushover.
Still, for that I'm grateful.

Now you stammer, 'we-eell....'
kindness returns to air
as it might, as I fear forgetting.

It's the timbre for young women,
pretty ones from the papers,
me, at the right end
of a stay.

*

Months later. You've already flown
the post-exit-pre-arrival lounge –
the oompapa's only a feud
with yourself and English clouds,
now you've been slowly restored
to earlier intentions: the youth
whose present to his mum was

two blue antique glasses,
one which said REMEMBER on it,
the other, ME, in white dots.

Joder (Sp.); fuck

Pigeon

I almost trip; riff-raff,
tipped, punch drunk with death,
he tumbles out. A spurt
of flighty blood diverts
rat-tail feet from dizzy
rings – he careens and lists
mid-road, collides with hope
through bikes and cars as though
you made him up, lifts off,
lift off... tenebrous, soft,
his flight deceives the sky
it's full of life.

The Accomplice

Unlikelihood was a sign,
their thresholds, say, entrances
of brutalist high-rises on the school run.
But you could've told us anything.

We leave the multi-storey car park,
with engine off, eyes tight shut
(against the deadness of our mother),
enter where eternals hide her,

gliding with that sense of flashing –
guided through the lurch from rushing
into the vortex of their portal
and warmth from unearthly laws.

Rush hour traffic, seconds later,
glitters on in orange rain.

Sunday's end was always lighter
slid outside of for a moment,
this world: optional.

Thrush

The headlong stumble –
you feel dumber, ivy trembles.
The same just older thrush,
thrust upwards from sheer...
sheerer...

Later, such clear silver branches
are criss-crossed
where someone's red-hot bouquet
tumbled against an alien quiet.

At the roots a papoose of words, more roses,
not supposed to live or die.
It makes us voyeurs of ourselves.

The thrush returns.
Ebullience. It wipes us out.

At Last

No. It was never white-to-blacker-
than-pitch. All your shades flickered
on and off, in different arrangements,
for years.

Do you remember those spoons
you gave me like a bunch of flowers?
The gilded Handbooks to Cathedrals
(they bored me – now they catch my throat)?

Hurt, behind your own, more savage, pen?

The window is mirroring
a study that you never entered.
But the sweetest man is knocking from
the deepest room I locked him in.

He asks me to be freed –
not that I should free him.

On the Edge of the Field

In diasporic cadences,
birds bash it home like ghosts –
everything hangs in the air: a shitter
in plain view, shouts, explodes
or implodes. Unravelling un-souled guts
is rabbit machinery outed by kites:
then dazzled by birth, trailing the burst
inner house, a cow rasps dry her fly-ridden calf.
The bubble-strewn field whirls towards
the rip, and sounds of honey, gathering.

Tiny Thistles

Love felt animal, undestroyable
for anything up to several hours
when you smiled me welcome there.

I'm lying on marjoram, thistles
hugging our chalk escarpment.
No angle unveils
the view's real colours.

Settling on words brings its sensations,
prickles like dishonesty
to you, me, the worlds between us –

yet there's a need to weld the dead's
irreconcilable parts. A last
effort to grasp, before it's too late,
what's ungraspable, bubble-man. Babbo.
Dad.

III

Tracks on the Skin

The past, loose on its rails from dust
joins with tickles from modern breezes.

Potent in nondescript spaces,
lights still haunt what's kept under wraps,
a pine spikes with resin tears...
uneasy silences when heat
buzzed to white even seas,
force through anodyne seasons.

Being a 'die-hard romantic' is how some excuse
an educated lack of trust.

But skin's map was never a signpost,
only marking what has passed –
that may yet be disavowed.

Glimmer

You glimpse, say, metallics,
threads, colours, fabric,
or perhaps glass. Tin.
Anything. Glittering
tights... on the edges
of sight, as if before meanings
killed them – remember

the alien glamour of certain
patterns known like beasts,
bodily: fused to taste,
smell, hearing. Fairyland.
Sex, before it existed.

You blink. Contextual again.
Nothing.
The present has gobbled them.

Beech Wood

Stopped on the track mid echo of screams –
mewls of hawks, clipping the tree tops –
not for that, but for gaps in what's read as a wood
(could be roe deer, muntjac or the loaded
breath of the dead and rotted-down
held to itself, weighing down),
we hear quiet restored to leaves drifting,
bloating one creak, a snap; that instant relief
from gold bars twinkling.

Mr Charles Brown and his Horse, Back from Market

At vanishing point
where ash and crab-apple hoop-frame
a dazzle of unfailing light,
the past isn't lost.

Before the cast who beckons us
is slashed by a shush from speeded-up
cars, and just out of sight,
the revenants change:

from Up Somborne a two-wheeled cart.
It creeps up in rhythms of wood-creak and iron-
on-wet. A last turnip, rolling.
The jingle of harness
patterning silence, forsaken chickweed.

No Van Gogh brights for you, Mr Brown,
but sun streak on wood mouse, leaf.
Dried blood for the wheels.

And you, you turn back to dapple.
You're deep in the tangle of underground roots,
tripping us backwards on tracks like these.
Back in the fabric of witnessing trees.

Poem commissioned by Jack Thacker, Poet-in-Residence at MERL, Reading, to be hung alongside the late-19th century market cart of Charles Brown from Up Somborne, Hants.

Apologia

We were in that paradoxical city
of locked-in souls and pioneers
watering your greenhouse pimientos.
Beyond a no-man's-land, yellow salsify,
the Goans next door barbecued two fish.
A wild cat watched how we convinced ourselves
this was doing the trick, when really the air
was thick with an ease that seemed outside our grasp,
then notes of unidentifiable grief
that billowed round flats on heatwave thermals.
I had to believe we existed in others' eyes,
didn't know how to break the spell
and free us.

Delusions of Grandeur

Walled in by lumpen hedges,
I dream of my childhood friend
here home from real-life death.

Cocteau-esque, silvered,
he slips into the stream
once fed by adolescent love
('negligence' has forced him).
Amid clothes, limbs,
his face is blurred, ineffable.

We'll safen his ending through sex, I imagine,
though he seems oblivious
to my soon permanent loss.

Mercurial surfaces, everything, moves.
In monochrome, glimpsed,
our profiles' loose entanglement
alludes to true release.

Dream Flight

After Corvus, Auriga, Vega,
I look up the 'Double Double'
where we are now,
the flair between hitched-up stars,
all words that reached this reader
of yours.

Being a mere dreamer, I need their
embodiment too.
Can I soar over Rue des Saints Pères,
lured by your roof under cloud,
steer through our separations:
air, slate, blood,
tongue, glass, stone –

land on rhomboids of platinum...
peer at your face, the half mirror in it,
how we will up and disappear?

There will be all those spaces
you named not-naming, between us, also,
your trickle of winter.

Good Dream

I told you I'd done many,
many, worse things that nobody knew.
Nothing said could come between us.
Pliant in thanked arms,
you let me pluck at your hair

which made us both feel air-light.
(Odd, that list you recited,
what weighed on your mind;
it was a breeze to soothe such fears.)

I woke to the true impasse,
a secret ice-cave in the gut,
the hectic buzz
of silences.
Greenhouses of empty air
where blind expectations were.

Then tits flew at the windows,
not light, instead small stanchions
of sameness.
Like them, I stuck with the daylight's suggestions,
recalled those conclusions
strung on the winds. Like burst balloons.

Stamped on the Day

Insistent, this dawn
beleaguered thunder and lightning
that crackled the forms night took;
on its grey back, the torn
business of living clambers,
earth invisibly quakes
inside a littered cloak,
tickled close to death by us.

Our motivation blacks
the curved horizon.
Back-slapping strikes the long
hour, the lacks stink, slack
in their networks;
how to get up, think?
How to get up, blink –

and just a small fragment of night
that was silvered and blasted us back
remains. It hangs like a crack
in an eye full of floaters and light.
Like a way out, stamped on the day.

Under the Supermoon

Nada te turbe, nada te espante

1.

What a furore, pre-perigee syzygy.
Displacement activity? Innocence?

No *sizzle* in the slink and silvered chinks of this;
larded, it slurs arrhythmic loaded nights.
Tribologist – of obsidian waves, warheads, peoples –
it elides invisible fauna, shivering thicknesses
of blues. Stalwart above a newness it can't discern,
it leads us, but as a dream does, coldly.
Caresses as it braces us
for the world's longer slow in-breath.

2.

This shriek's unformed by teeth and tongue –
cross between a laying hen
and some hoarse interrogation
that knows it is unanswerable.

I've no idea who runs along
the frost-burnt field; what streaks its longing
star-wards – nor how that echo echoes ours.

'*Nada te turbe, nada te espante*' (Sp.); 'Let nothing disturb you, let nothing frighten you'. St Teresa of Avila

From Surd to Love

Irrational. On breath, not voice
(ssss, ttttt, ffff). Surd (numbers)
from *alogos* (Greek): speechless
and irrational,

the Latin *Surdus*: (deaf, silent,
stupid) via *jadhr asamm*,
Arabic for deaf root.
Or from Surd, Hungary

(possibly). Then susurrus.
Absurd: (philosophical)
conflict between the human urge
for meaning and the lack of it.

Irrational, breath, not voice,
hungry amongst the voiceless leaves:
this root.

Before & Thirty Years On

On our small island, between
Boulevard de Clichy and Rue Lepic,
it rains for weeks. Lilac clouds
soak white and purple lilac flowers,
the *vitrier* screams about panes of glass.
The place is threaded
with white and lilac vertical lines;
a brushed sky, fat on slated roofs,
makes threnodies I take for
more iconic melodies – assuming
she'll stick with life.

*

Hurt torched your voice to darkness in dreams.
Yet you're quieter these days, appear
not drowning, or in scenarios
where I'm the dud rescuer
of our lives. Examining this fire's
efficient flames, how in one hiss
a leaf's extinguished, I can't desire
to rid myself of your suffering,
since that's how you make yourself known.
In fact I fear forgetting
its toxic glow under my skin.

Falling Out of Love (Towards Love)

Above a lemon treeline
today some flitty bird
sparks off a wedge of cloud.
Snow has got this secretive.

It is not yet snowing
where I half invented you,
opens like a ripened view,
clearer than this liar's bed,
quieter than a symptom.

On the low horizon
the flitty bird has gone.
Snow comes in with dull
layers from your weather
examined with my glasses on.

Leo

What you missed was by a
whisker.

As if I were swimming
but through a rough skid, my lids
refused to shutter my eyes.
Some beauty is razor wire

(your Malian kora teacher
on air – today, years later,
even Trio Da Kali) –
yet sounds like your élan, survivor.

*

In the privilege of quiet,
candlelight – the softest wind.
You have left
and left the accumulated
effort of our long task
intact in the house.
You are safe tonight. That is enough.
Incessant, the flame
sparks on an incoming draft
this Christmas Eve.

*

There are no birds, only bruises
tumbling over lemon,
at earth's loadline, cranes, high-rises
(charcoaled-in by a long-dead friend
years before this love was born).

Dare I imagine being your skin,
under a skin too awoken...
yet we are here, now aligning
between two deep reservoirs,
swept down the causeway by freer winds,
you re-skinned, in another name.

IV

True Story

It never became a story, that scene –
leaves, a film-noir blur in the car roofs,
wind full of chestnuts, a smart tattoo in the score.

2 am. Their limousine's a purr and
levelling crunch on grit, the girl chauffeur's
slamming a leathered door.

He weighs on her neck, unseen,
hauls his poor withered legs
across to wide steps.

Well lit, he might be twenty-four,
is candle white.

They fall inside like illicit bank notes.
Sliding glass seals them in the dark
Hôtel de L'Espérance.

Stopped

She didn't marry for madness,
this stranger-to-himself,
wonders at her own health.
And settling back in dark's
recent malevolence
anything might happen;

her car is no benign
holding, the lay-by's blowing
with paper cups and crisps,
while those speeding oases
are further than the green
and red brilliance
of stars.

Where are the edges
of too dangerous,
when do you jump?

Girl on Motorway Bus

She watches (like a dish
of silver, mirror-thin)
a filigree of brides
branching rain veils
(cherries blossoming
in unknown lengths, green umber),
a scumbled bird-hued hill
over acid rape.

Some people, like the man
who took to visiting,
stand, backs to the landscape,
stomachs full of themselves.
Neither are well, she supposes,
preferring her kind for
pictures flashed off them.

The Festival Poet

For Pedro Serrano

Different whites of skin
in winter fields.
Surviving wipers, cadences.
And what's not revealed
through disguise of face
tightened by their thrown-rose kisses.

By nightfall his lips were beleaguered.
Un-ironic stars, an after-hours Marine Bar,
found us familiar.

A juggernaut is overtaking.
Curled in snow-filled clouds, again
his poems' burnt edge.

Lived between two coasts,
old grief like ours was neither here nor there.

Guests at a Book Launch

Like before-to-imagined
pictures of missing people
lots have superimposed age

To some we are once-scribbled-down stories,
half remembered, or
flicked through ex-arousals,
let go again at the end –

yet drift inside denouements
as if thumbnail sketches done
from genuine affection
by an absent friend.

At the Plant Stall, February 2017

Trumpets versus
bleeding hearts.
Acidanthera.
Yellow baskets.

This winter of lush
blank page after page's
scribbled on garishly
by shocking weather.

They're coming up hardened,
tired of sick winds;
narcissi, stunted
cyclamen.

Yet the choiceless
spring persists. Irresistible.
Sweetness....

City Fragments, February 2018

… something circus-y in these
oompapas.
Air's between early spring
& blood boiling over.

You'd think he was kipping, but look,
the rough-sleeper's shoeless
toe wags along, through saps un-shed.

The old guys
have us all speeding.
Try not to walk in time,

jump to shrieks that are only laughter.
A siren.
On a canary strip the evening star winks.

Things bubble 'stop!'
on a distant continent.
Radar pulses (evolution) under the skin.

Two Writers Walking
For Chris Baines

… so we pick over an absence
of feedback. Young pheasants stick
where marjoram's gridded
by mesh barriers,
then scuttle up sides of the valley
in a mouse-brown flood,
like stumbling kids.

We pick over ghostings,
blips in transmission herded on airwaves
as they hop onto five-bar gates,
tumble on upwards
in the sights of men trained on each stage:
what's still penned up, released,
ready to be blasted. Freed.

Lights in the Departure Lounge

Blue-green, and more alone for choosing grand,
a lit-up girl leans down towards her screen,
while fixed on somewhere else, with laptop bags,
a cruising pod of muted Japanese
derails her glassy restaurant mise-en-scène
and everyone is framed inside a frame of mind.
So this is how you're taken in
by old man skin, an antique gleam, a space
that opens out from him, and might be traced by memory
to pink cathedral stone
or desert sand you've known, perhaps.
His face has never parted from the bones of land.
He turns to a companion:
one moonbeam to complete this feel of home.

After the Service

For L.B.

In the falling and slow caving in,
sheer glitter of components,

you bore flowers from her name,
her lateral dimensions

a casket closed on her.

That noun belongs to old order.

Adamantine,
daylight follows one more night

and this pavement's stiff
with privilege and sparkle.

You'll set out like a skiff –
it's a one-person passage

(the only option's been taken).

But this is my memory leaking
on your undecipherable cracks

and unreadable networks
binding.

V

Outside a Florist's, mid-December

Aligned against the wall, they're slumped.
Tilted. Like pigs fattened for us,
then killed. And as if, in this interim
high winds might just remind them –
their resinous ghosts – of one kind of freedom,
they bristle in loose nets.
As if, in limbo, Christmas trees
might break free and kill us
for the beauty of our bodies
when encumbered with their thoughts.

The Rabbit I Tamed Yawns

She opens doors on intimate designs
like these along her jaw-line
or soil tamped down beside the hole –
or red stained urine of hard winters,
rotten crab apple burnt through snow.

She tucks away untidy bones.
Puffed-up shades of shadowed reeds, back-lit,
silver guard hairs' shiver round her.
Egyptian eyes glint river-black.
Reverberations rock and shift,
reconfigure her.

From Watlington Hill

As each plane bombs along trajectories
machines have mapped, those cluttering chalk marks,
one well-proportioned cross, drift
then shred, to wisps. *'Aleppo is hours
into another broken ceasefire'*.
Kites wheel. Their screaming is silent
from that height. It's a quiet
scene of dog-walkers out with their pets,
none of whom seem to smell dread.

Between the Lines
(Traces from a Small Tractor)

While you see pelvic shadows, platysmas, perhaps
in chalkland, gazing from Britwell
behind dark bells and barrels of sheep
a matrix of queasy symmetry
encases a swell of widening ribs.
It's like Ravilious' high-strung heartbeat
further excited by recent advances.

Then paler, like ghosted,
free-wheeling lines crossing the track marks
make out a driver veered off to elsewhere
just as the cursive script of a daydream
plays along these dead straight lines,
then leaps...

The Sponsored Ride

Where our footpath kinks,
this logjam. Hijacked breaths
articulate steam ghosts...
clattering anxiety.

Strings are pulled.
They can't fall apart, must shorten.

Grey lips flinch, furl
up messages. They're safest
silencing stabs of discomfort.

We lean back, into brambles.
Threaded flesh sparks as it passes,
naked as newly peeled chestnut.

Then they're distanced, cut-outs.
Uccello colours crown the escarpment –
reds, white, brown,
the black trees over disquieted fields.

Dead Tree Amongst Memorials

For Harriet and Simon Frazer

Amidst rook trajectories,
a bluster and bricolage
of blue-black words for outrage
settling in low-slung eddies

your ash's antlers jig
some kind of bony cipher
(shadowed lines on Kodak sky),
distance gloss tresses between them

call for words to be hung
like small banners, like meanings
allowed to drift towards dying
and reform.

After Restoring the Name on a Grave
To E.A.

We can't guess the trees' end,
how papery cases twist against dulled wheat.
Our over-bright selves
steal under skies emptied of light
by these hungry lines. The flickers are seeds'
slow-matured silvers. They will get eaten.

Drifting, the midges
disappear.
Straight paths swallow uncertainty,
white paths, suspicious sparks.
An army of heads and dizzying chevrons
points up the hedges as
premature shouts.

What startles sets out like cloud-scud
or eels – faster now, minnows.
Bent on crop ears
they pool in ellipses, dips.
Diminish, slow, like wind-chart arrows.

But the stone thrown into their pond
is only subsiding breeze.

Notes from Aldeburgh Beach

1. Christmas Tree

For the survivors

It's camped in saline winds'
gull cradle, points
up, numb, obedient...

A blink away from summer,
sun's winter platinum
drapes seas' disturbances

arriving at this fir
someone planted so far
from soil, forest, songbirds.

2016 ends
here, with rounded pebbles,
one beam, a tall triangle

as if in that early tingle
when hope makes itself known
such geometry might become
each lost figure in a picture of peace.

2. Autumn 2017

There is no note here
to colour its fidget and blur.
Opaline
from relating to sun,
it dims horizon's
vast slow-moving ghost.
Sucked in shingle,
plash of hushed wavelets, pass on
inhuman song,
deaf to us humans
who made 'inhuman' sin.

In Gratitude

To certain poets

… Because the countries
are not ours, but almost
the very same we lost,
and borderless

travel is a gift
to sufferers.
Because you see a glass
trembling the city's

light-webs, not knowing how
a few words do this –
how, to half-buried souls,
being uncovered
might feel like love.

Two Rivers Press has been publishing in and about Reading since 1994. Founded by the artist Peter Hay (1951–2003), the press continues to delight readers, local and further afield, with its varied list of individually designed, thought-provoking books.

The poems in this collection are set in Janson – a lively modern revival of a traditional serif typeface with high stroke contrast and a large x-height to aid legibility. For the headings, we've used Parisine, a contemporary sanserif, to provide a counterpoint to the classic feel of Janson, and to distinguish notes and epigraphs from the poems.